Superhuman YOU:

Break The Chains of Limitations and Unleash Your Own Superpower!

IRON TAMER DAVE WHITLEY

ISBN: 9781530669424

DEDICATION

Being a strongman is an unusual way to live, to say the least. I can only imagine what it must be like being married to a strongman. Purchases of large quantities of steel and horse shoes. Destroyed kitchen wear. Shredded pieces of poker cards getting into the sofa cushions. Bruises. Occasional phone calls that you need a ride to the ER to get stitches.

This book is dedicated to my wife Mandy for her love and support through everything.

TABLE
OF
CONTENTS

Acknowledgments   vii

INTRODUCTION   1

TOWARD   3
SUPERHUMAN

1 STUTTERING   5
CHILD BECOMES
SUPERHUMAN

2 BENDING STEEL   11

3 STRONG MAN -   17
STRONG MIND

4 STRENGTH   29
BEYOND
STRENGTH

5 BEGIN WHERE YOU   35
ARE

6 WHAT IS SUCCESS?   39

7 DEEPER   45
UNDERSTANDING

8 THOUGHT   53

9 THE PROCESS   63

10 DEVELOPING   97
    YOUR SUPER
    POWER

    CONCLUSION   117

    ABOUT THE   119
    AUTHOR

ACKNOWLEDGMENTS

To my dad Gene Whitley and my late mother Frances for alway believing in me and encouraging me to be what I wanted to be, no matter how outlandish it seemed at the time.

I owe much gratitude the following folks, who have contributed to my knowledge of strength and the power of the mind. Without them this book wouldn't exist: Dennis Rogers, Slim the Hammer Man Farman, Bud Jeffries, Jedd Johnson, Chris Rider, Adam Glass, Pat Povilaitis, Eric Vining, James Alexander, Eric Moss, Joe Vitale, Bob Proctor.

Thanks to Dennis Breckey, Sean McLellan, Mark Brown, Ida Zapichi, Bre Sprague and Terriane Palmer-Peacock for input, ideas and helping me bring the vision of this book into reality.

INTRODUCTION

by Joe Vitale

In my career so far, I've been able to meet several actors who played superhuman characters. I met Dean Cain who played Superman. And I met Lou Ferrigno who played the Hulk. These people are very healthy, very wise, and very athletic, but they're not superhuman. They were actors.

I've been on a search to find out how you become superhuman. How do you increase your mind power? How do you increase your physical power? I've been reading books that promised mind power and strength since I was a kid. But they never seemed to get to the sacred point of superhuman.

And then I discovered Iron Tamer Dave Whitley. He taught me some things that have been unforgettable. I can now bend nails, bolts, steel bars and horseshoes. You haven't lived until you felt the juice that comes from bending a horseshoe in your bare hands. It makes you feel, well, superhuman.

I am learning more feats of strength. Why? Because they build inner confidence. They build outer strength. And they give me that feeling of superhuman powers that I was seeking.

I'm almost like a comic book superhero who has come to life in this reality we all share. I wish I knew some of these secrets fifty years ago, when I was an insecure youngster being picked on by others.

This book is truly a phenomenon. It will inspire you. It will inform you. And it will help you tap into your superhuman abilities. Right now that might feel like a stretch but it's true. It's possible to do more than you ever imagined.

And it all begins now when you turn the page...

Joe Vitale
A star in the movie The Secret
Author of way too many books to list here
Strongman in Training
www.JoeVitale.com

TOWARD SUPERHUMAN

Why do we have such a fascination with super heroes? I believe it is because we see the best qualities of ourselves in them. They are exaggerated version of what we all aspire to be.

I grew up wanting to be a super hero, or more specifically, wanting to have superhuman powers. It may sound like a bold claim, but I achieved that desire. I bend steel bars with my hands.

I am convinced that every single one of us on planet Earth has the ability to become super human. We each have at least one unique super power. A power that can change the course of our own lives and the lives of those around us.

Just like in the comic books, any super power can be used for good or for evil. It all depends on the mindset of the one who wields the power. The power can be used to help us live a success-filled and happy life. Or it can can cause us to spiral into a chaotic world of pain and misery.

My hope is that as you go through this book, you will discover and develop the unique super power that exists in you and that you will you use it to make the world around you a better place.

1
STUTTERING CHILD
BECOMES SUPERHUMAN

I was born in Nashville, Tennessee in November of 1969.

As a kid, I alternated between chubby and downright fat. To make matters worse I had a horrible stutter. It was so bad that I would get physically ill if I had to get in front of the class and speak for something like a book report, even though I loved to read.

Early on I was exposed to dinosaurs, myths of the Norse and Greco/Romans and of course I also developed a fondness for comic books and cartoons, Spiderman, Godzilla, King Kong…you know, normal boy stuff. I was naturally extroverted, but the fact that I could barely get two words out of my mouth in front of a group of people put a bit of a damper on things. I was bullied, picked on and made fun of by many of the other kids, for both being fat and for stuttering. I spent a lot of time feeling "different" and being angry at other kids my age and also at myself because I couldn't figure out how to fit in with them. More and more I retreated into fantasy land, where I could pretend I had super powers.

I was always fascinated by super strength and other super human abilities, so any character in comics or myth that displayed great strength quickly became a favorite.

Enter the Hulk. More specifically, Enter Lou Ferrigno. Here was a multiple-time Mr. Universe-turned-TV-actor portraying the Green Goliath on the small screen every week. By age seven, I had claimed the Hulk as a favorite, no doubt due to his anger and rage powering his mighty strength, making him the "Strongest one there is!"

Reading the comics and using my imagination to enter into that world was awesome. But seeing Ferrigno, onscreen and painted green, bring humanity to the character had an effect on my young mind and spirit that has lasted to this very moment. I can still vividly recall the feeling I had the night the pilot aired and the first transformation occurred as Dr. David Banner lost control of his emotions changing a tire in a thunderstorm. I imagined what it must feel like to be possessed of a strength and power that allowed him to bend steel and lift heavy things.

Seeing Ferrigno onscreen, my child's mind knew that this was a man in makeup, playing a role. At that moment, seeing him in all his Hulkish glory, it became possible in my mind for a person to be big, strong and mighty.

Like the Hulk.

This was critical…. a pivotal moment for me. Because in that moment what was once a fantasy, inspired by comic book and cartoon, became a very real **possibility**. Prior to that moment, fantasy was fantasy, imagination was different than reality and I was unaware that reality could be molded by imagination. As Slim the Hammer Man would tell me decades later "If one man can do it, another man can do it. And if another man can do it, I can certainly do it."

My parents encouragement and admonition that I could "Do or be anything I wanted" took on a whole new meaning.

Watching Ferrigno on TV, it became possible in my young child mind that very night to become not just strong, but to have super human strength.

I could actually become SUPER HUMAN.

It was a a lifelong game-changer. There was just one detail that presented a snag; I had no absolutely idea how to proceed.

Taking what I knew of superhuman abilities from the world of comics, science fiction and fantasy, I began to explore and eliminate options in my young mind. I considered being bombarded with high levels of gamma radiation, but had no idea where to go to get that done, since this was in the days before the internet.

I also thought about being bitten by radioactive spiders and traveling into space to expose myself to the mysterious "cosmic rays" I had read about in comics. Again, I was unable to secure the resources I needed.

I looked all over the woods near my house for fallen meteors that would most certainly give me the powers I sought, but it was to no avail. Reading books and comics about Tarzan and Conan, I thought that maybe I missed my chance because I was not raised by apes or born on an ancient battlefield.

Then one night on PBS, the movie "Pumping Iron" was broadcast. It must have been around 1980 or so, because not only was the Incredible Lou Ferrigno in this movie (as his human self!) but so was Arnold Schwarzenegger, who was the actor in the Conan the Barbarian movie. I paid very little attention to the plot, but I remember being fascinated, absolutely transfixed by the images of the monstrous muscle men during the training segments. The huge weights they moved. The effort of their intensity. The sweat and screams as they went to battle and made WAR on the iron.

This was the key. Lifting things gave you the ability to lift heavy things, and lifting heavy things gave you the ability to lift even heavier things. A pattern had emerged that revealed to my child mind a simple truth of cause and effect. There was no need for any gamma bombs or radioactive spiders. I now knew how those guys had become so big and strong.

That was it. I announced that night that I was going to become super-strong and huge and that the number one item on my Christmas list was a set of weights. The thought, the desire, was all-consuming. I saw the weights as a tool to develop the strength I coveted.

My father, who was quite strong from working as a carpenter when he wasn't playing music professionally, taught me about pushups and pull-ups. They were quite difficult for me as I was still beyond chubby. These simple bodyweight exercises were the snack to hold me over until Santa arrived with my concrete and plastic adjustable barbell/dumbbell set and weight bench.

I set the weights up in my room and immediately started curling and pressing, like I had seen in Pumping Iron. Every few minutes I would stop to flex in the mirror to see if the swoleness (which is a term that I am fairly certain wasn't even invented yet) had appeared and wondering why after a few days of training I didn't yet look like Louie or Arnold.

And so it began.

Eventually....decades later......I would discover that to become a true-life superhuman, for me, meant that I would become a performing strongman. Furthermore, I would come to understand that all of us are born with the potential to become superhuman. We need only accept it. Once we accept our own superhuman potential, we can begin to discover and develop our own unique super powers.

These super powers are the key to greatness and while it may not be super strength or the ability to fly or being a human spider that is your super power, I assure you that you have one. Perhaps it is a musical talent. Or the ability to invent something that doesn't exist yet. It doesn't have to be fantastic. It only has to be a full expression of YOU.

That is the subject matter of almost all my performances as a strongman. It is also the reason I decided to write this book.

By the time you finish this book, you will be introduced to the unlimited power of potential that you have. You will have a clear idea in your mind of how to proceed in developing it.

You will be on your way to becoming superhuman.

2
BENDING STEEL:
THOUGHT IN ACTION

I have read many, many books on the subject of the human mind and thought, in particular the idea that many refer to as the Great Secret: **We become what we think about.**

We all have our own understanding of this, and since this is my book, I am going to share with you my own perspective. I promise that it is not just another "think happy thoughts" kind of book, although there is definitely an element of that.

I will present this information, as I understand it, from the perspective of an performing strongman.

What is a performing strongman?

What does a performing strongman do?

How does he do it?

Most importantly, what does that have to do with you, the reader?

I am glad you asked. In the late 1800s and early 1900s the term strongman was used to refer to someone who performed exhibition of various feats of strength, usually onstage in Vaudeville or the circus. Because of this history, the term performing strongman is synonymous with "old-time strongman" today. I use them interchangeably.

The old-time strongman performances often included feats such as bending steel bars and horse shoes, breaking chains, etc. These feats demanded a great deal of bodily power, often emphasizing strength of the wrist and hands. Obviously, this form of entertainment stills exists, and I am proud to be an old-time performing strongman.

How do we do the things we do? There is a great amount of physical training involved, for sure. But what I want to share with you is the more important mental aspect of how we accomplish the impossible.

Some of these strongmen, most notably Joseph Greenstein whose stage name was the Mighty Atom, also pursued strength as a means of mental and spiritual development and refinement. I agree with this approach and fully embrace it in my own life.

I am a fan of clear definitions. One definition of being strong is the possession of strength and we typically use the word *strong* as an adjective and pair it with other words: Strong body, strong will, strong wind blowing, etc.

We tend to think of the physical first, but being *strong* (possessing *strength*) is something that goes beyond the physical performance of feats or lifts and encompasses the entire being. It is a means of discovering, unifying and expressing the True Self. This is my personal definition of it, and this is my book, so I get to make that call. ;-)

In addition to lifting and feats of strength, my own strength practice has included physical and breathing exercises from martial arts, chi kung and yoga for over 20 years now.

The word *yoga*, translated from Sanskrit literally means *union*. Translated from Japanese the word *kaizen* literally means *good change*. The similarity of these words/ideas with the idea of strength is very clear to me. As the old saying goes, there are many paths up the mountain, the view from the top is the same.

Strength training is the act of willingly expressing the spirit. The word *dojo* is a Japanese term which literally means "place of the way". My good friend Dustin Rippetoe was the first person that I ever heard use the term Way of Strength. In the expression of the Spirit is where I believe our superhuman ability lies.

There is strength in the body. There is strength in the emotions. There is immense strength in wisdom and love and compassion. The pursuit and development of strength, in its most complete form, establishes a union for all parts of the individual and moves one in the direction of continual improvement in all areas. Physical power, health, peace, happiness, wisdom, love, wealth, abundance and prosperity: When I say to you "Be Strong", I am wishing all theses things to you.

As you can see, my approach to strength runs deeper than picking up heavy things or bending steel. By pursuing the development of strength in body, mind, breath and energy, we wind up focusing our practice into the deeper arena of the awareness of the Self. This is what I mean when I tell folks that bending steel is a meditative practice.

There are many, many approaches to building strength. Instead of strictly adhering to a way of thought as the "Only True Way", we must understand and apply ideas and principles in a way that lines up with the goal at hand. This is a very personal thing, both in terms of a specific physical goal and even more so in the expression of Self. Ultimately I am concerned with one thing: Doing what works to achieve the goal. Why? Because therein lies Truth.

Strength is a foundational quality. When it improves, everything else tends to improve with it. The practice of getting stronger in the gym or Dojo (wherever it may be) gives way to a strengthening of the integration of body, mind and spirit. We can develop - one lift at a time- the awareness of not only our present strength, but also our **potential strength.** It is here that the more profound benefits of our training become apparent.

The ability to recognize that being stronger enhances everything, in all situations, allows us to redefine possibilities in our lives and understand how we can become the strongest, most fulfilled version of our Self. Through the practice of getting stronger, we learn to move better, feel better, think more clearly, enjoy situations more fully. We learn to endure unpleasant things in a more accepting way. We understand gratitude and freedom more fully as our strength grows.

If we think of strength as an attitude to be developed rather than a physical quality, then the beautiful fact is that it is left open for interpretation by and expression of, the individual. "Strong" may not mean the same thing to me as it does to you in the physical sense of a heavy deadlift or tearing a deck of cards, for example, but the act of being strong and the road travelled in its pursuit is a common thread to all of us.

My interpretation is concerned with freedom of the spirit and the expression of self.

It is about discarding the idea that we must be forced into established little boxes for the convenience or approval of someone else.

It is about waking up deeper levels of self awareness and expressing ourselves with the fullness that we deserve. It is about refining and re-defining.

It is about becoming.

When I perform feats of strength, I continue a tradition that was laid down by my mentors and their mentors. I seek to honor these "ancestors" by carrying their traditions forward into a new age. Seeking to blend together the knowledge of both the old-timers and modern approaches provides a balance to the practice. The essence of strength remains unchanging, but must be adapted to meet the practitioner where they are in order to move toward it.

Be Strong.

3

STRONG MAN, STRONG MIND

Ask any performing strongman and they will tell you that mindset is the key to everything we do. Without the right attitude, without confidence, bending steel spikes and horse shoes is not going to happen. It truly is as much (or even more) mind than muscle.

There have been many strength athletes who have influenced my thinking over the years. From Ferrigno and Arnold when I was a child all the way until today.

Warren Lincoln Travis using a special padded ring, lifted 667lb. with one finger.

Hermann Goerner, who performed a 727lb Deadlift. With one hand!

Arthur Saxon and his incredible overhead lift of 370lbs. Also done with one hand!

But there are three strongmen who have influenced me the most and they are a direct lineage. Without them, I would not be doing feats of strength.

THE MIGHTY ATOM

An incredibly inspiring example of this is one of my favorite strongmen, Joseph Greenstein, The Mighty Atom. (seen here bending a horse shoe with his teeth)

He is credited with one of my favorite all time favorite quotes:

"Never limit yourself by the seemingly impossible. Place no limits upon yourself and you will have none. Think that you are strong...and you are."

The Atom was only 5 feet 5 inches tall and weighed 145lbs, but he is without question one of the greatest strongmen who ever walked the earth. His philosophy was that to perform any feat required that he must first succeed in his mind. Mind and spirit.....then action....like a bullet fired from a gun, once it begins, it is already done.

This approach served him well in the area of strength feats. He was one of the greatest when it came to bending steel bars, spikes and horse shoes. He would drive a nail through a board and several pieces of tin with his palm and only a small piece of cloth as padding.

Many of these kinds of feats are still done by today's strength performers, myself included. Every time I bend a spike or drive a nail though a board, I am thankful to be carrying on the tradition of the Mighty Atom.

In his lifetime, the Atom did many things that would be truly considered impossible. Things that, as far as I know, no other strongman has ever duplicated.

On at least 2 occasions, he stopped airplanes from moving. With his hair.

He regularly bit nails and chains in half. That is not a typo. He bit them. They separated into two pieces. I have seen the remnants of one such nail myself. It doesn't look cut or sawed, it looks bitten.

The Mighty Atom passed on from this existence in October of 1977, but his influence lives on in strongmen all over the world and will continue to do so.

His biography, written by Ed Spielman, was published in 1978. It is out of print now, but if you can find a copy of it and are interested in his full story, it is worth whatever you have to pay.

The Mighty Atom lived to be 83 years old and he performed feats of strength right up to the end. In the picture above, he is driving a nail through a board with his hand. He never considered his size, age or circumstance to be an obstacle. He understood that his superhuman abilities originated in his mind and were expressed through his body.

SLIM THE HAMMER MAN

Lawrence Farman, known as Slim the Hammer Man in strongman circles, is over 80 years old and has been a strongman since he was in his 20's and began study with the Mighty Atom.

Slim is the undisputed king of leverage lifting, having taken his mastery of it and turning it into a true art form. In the photo above, Slim is performing a lever lift with a 27lb axe on a 36 inch handle. If you math that out, it is roughly 972lbs of torque on the wrist.

SLIM THE HAMMER MAN

In this photo, he is doing a double hammer leverage lift totaling 56.5lbs.

When the Mighty Atom passed away in 1977, Slim became one of the last of the legendary old-time strongmen. Carrying on in the tradition and spirit of his mentor, he is a living testament to the superhuman power of the mind and body.

He has said this many times:

"It's not that you don't have the power; it's that you can't get to the power because of the fear. The power is already there, inside you. The question is, how can you bring it out?"

Slim is referring to the strength that we all have inside us, that shows up in the stories of untrained people doing heroic feats in times of emergency, like a mother lifting a car off her child. While many of these stories are urban legend, I have managed to find several that were factual. Incidentally, this inner strength, or rather the lack of it, was what led David Banner to subject himself to gamma rays in the Hulk TV series.

The good news is that you do not have to be put in a life and death situation in order to tap into your superpower. More on that later. For now I want to introduce you to another strongman, whom you may have seen on TV.

DENNIS ROGERS

My introduction to learning and performing feats of strength came about when I met my strongman mentor, Dennis Rogers. It was Dennis who taught me how to bend spikes, tear cards, twist horse shoes, roll up frying pans and a number of other feats. He is one of the very few men alive that can be considered a true Grandmaster Strongman. The only other person is Dennis' mentor, Slim the Hammer Man.

Like the Mighty Atom before him, Dennis looks very much like a normal guy at 5ft 8 inches and 170lbs. In the photo above, Dennis is curling a pair of hammers together that weigh 16lb and 20lbs and are not attached to each other. It's an uneven, unbalanced lift that is made even more difficult because he must squeeze the handles together to keep the hammers from flying apart.

One of his signature feats is driving a nail without a hammer. Slim also does this feat, as did the Mighty Atom. When I first learned to do this feat, it was absolutely terrifying. It has to be done with a tremendous amount of speed. Every time I attempted it, I could feel myself putting the brakes on and slowing down. I went to Texas and trained in person with Dennis and to his credit as a coach, he had me doing the feat successfully within a few minutes. He literally talked me through the fear of the danger and had me successfully driving the nail within a half hour.

Dennis, myself and Slim, 2012

In one interview I have with Dennis he said this:

"The reason people cannot do the things that we do is because they have put a limitation in their head and they have a fear that they cannot go past it or they will get hurt or feel pain. As strongmen, we don't think about that. We think about what we are gonna do and we just go there. Nothing is going to stop us."

At this point you may be thinking, "that is certainly interesting, fascinating and even inspiring."

But it still doesn't answer the most important question:

What does any of this have to do with YOU?

I believe that every single one of us has a yearning for expansion, a spark of desire to have, do or be in a better position than we are right now. I am certain that you are no exception.

With the strongmen I have mentioned, we see the vitally important recurring theme:

The body is the instrument of the mind.

The mind is what determines everything and the body is always subject to it. How else could a human do the impossible?

What I have found through the study of strong and successful people throughout history is that the process of excellence or mastery is universal, regardless of the desired outcome.

I have been a student and teacher of strength for many years. I often speak of "impossible as a job description". The cool thing about the impossible is that it is up to the individual to define it. What is impossible for one person is "just what you do on Thursday" for another.

In my opinion, impossible is simply a way to say that something hasn't been done yet.

On May 29th, 1953, Sir Edmond Hillary and Tenzing Norgay did the impossible and reached the summit of Mt. Everest. Hundreds of people have been there since.

Roger Bannister did the impossible in 1954 when he broke the barrier of the four minute mile. Over 1000 others have done it since then.

It doesn't only pertain to physical feats, either.

There was a time, not too long ago, that flight was impossible. On December 17, 1917, the Wright brothers changed that perception. Only 52 years later, man set foot on the moon.

These people all did something that not only had never been done, but that was widely believed could never BE done. And they are not that different from you.

I will describe, in detail, exactly how you can use the mind techniques I use to bend steel and twist horse shoes to achieve any goal you desire. It is the same process that produced the light bulb, space travel and the internet.

Slim the Hammer Man is 100% correct. You have the power in in you. A superhuman power that is just waiting to be expressed. Let's bring it out.

4
STRENGTH BEYOND STRENGTH

One day, my fascination with the concept of the body being an instrument of the mind showed up in a place that I didn't expect.

As a business owner and entrepreneur, I took it upon myself several years ago to learn as much as I could about how to grow a successful business in the fitness industry. I have owned and operated gyms and continue to travel all over the world performing and teaching.

One of the books that I read and began to seriously study was Napoleon Hill's classic *Think and Grow Rich.*

Hill was a student of Andrew Carnegie, who at the time was likely the richest man in the world. He was certainly one of the most powerful and influential. Carnegie believed that the process of achieving success could be outlined in a simple formula and that anyone at all could use that formula to attain any goal they truly desired. Carnegie put Hill to the task of compiling this information. Hill went on to interview, analyze and study the work and habits of over 500 successful men and women, including Thomas Edison, Henry Ford, Alexander Graham Bell and Theodore Roosevelt. In doing this he discovered and published this formula in various forms. The most well-known is the classic book, *Think and Grow Rich.*

As I got deeper into the study of Hill's material, I was struck by the familiarity contained in these quotes:

"Whatever a man can conceive and believe, he can achieve."

"Man, alone, has the power to transform his thoughts into physical reality. Man, alone, can dream and make his dreams a physical reality."

"The only limitations we have are those we set up in our own minds."

This sounded exactly like the teachings of the strongmen I had studied and emulated!

Inspired and curious, I went on to further investigate Napoleon Hill and many other great teachers of prosperity and abundance. Mind masters such as James Allen, author of *As A Man Thinketh* and Wallace Wattles who wrote *The Science of Getting Rich.*

I soaked up the recordings of Earl Nightingale, who did, among many other things, an audio condensation of *Think and Grow Rich.* I studied the programs of Bob Proctor, who I had first seen in the move *The Secret.*

I even wound up becoming friends with another star of *The Secret*, Dr. Joe Vitale. In fact it was Joe who challenged me not only to write this book but to bring it from thought to physical form in less than 90 days.

I had been taught imaging techniques by my mentors and practiced them countless times while training to do feats of strength. I use the term "imaging" because it goes beyond visualization. More than merely seeing myself perform the feat, I mentally rehearse it. I feel the steel in my hands. I smell the leather of my wraps and the chalk. I am fully "there" in my mind, even though my physical body is not performing the feat, my mind doesn't know the difference. Later in this book I will give you specific exercises that will help you to develop this skill in yourself.

With Joe Vitale, December 2015

Here were the greatest teachers of success telling me that the exact principles and methods that I was using to bend steel could be applied to successfully accomplish ANY objective, from earning money to health to improving relationships.

In my study and practice as a both strongman and a business owner, I had realized a connection.

There is quite literally a guiding principle that ties together both worlds. Not only that, I realized that it was a principle that guarantees success, no matter what the goal.

We become what we think about.

Once we truly understand this, then all we need do is think in the direction of the desired outcome. This is as certain as the law of gravity. But how do you put it to use?

Like most universal truths, it is simple to understand and execute. The difficult lies in our inherent human tendency to make things harder than they have to be. Simple and easy are not necessarily the same thing.

So, where do you start? And then, what do you do?

5
BEGIN WHERE YOU ARE

Let's start by taking an honest evaluation of where you are.

Perhaps you are not enjoying the amount of success you would like to have in any given area of your life. Maybe you want to bend steel. Maybe you don't.

Maybe you don't have the money you would like, or aren't in the kind of physical shape you want to be in. Maybe your relationships are lacking.

Maybe you spend time just going through the motions of life and wondering how you got to be in the position you are in.

This is the first place most of us get stuck: trying to figure out how we got there in the first place.

Was it our parents?

Our genetics?

The neighborhood we grew up in?

Some previous relationship?

We want to know why we got lost. We want to know why we are not doing as well as we want. But the truth is, how you got there doesn't matter.

What you do next does.

I already said this, but the most critical thing that you can take away from this book is this:

We become what we think about.

Your current results exist because of your past conditioning and the decisions that came as a result of that conditioning. Put another way, your current results are a manifestation of your past thoughts and behaviors. It doesn't matter how or why you got that conditioning. Nothing can change the past.

However, it is imperative that you understand this: Your current results are NOT an indicator of your present potential or of your future possibility. Your task now, if you truly want to improve your life, is to change the conditioning of your mind. You cannot change the past, but you can change your mental programming into whatever you want it to be.

In other words: If you are unhappy with the way you are, it is not your fault. It IS your fault if you stay that way.

You cannot get new results with old behavior patterns. You can only make permanent changes by changing your thoughts about yourself and the world around you. If you want new results, you MUST change the way you think. If you want superhuman results, you must begin to think like a superhuman.

36

This is critical. The way you think is either the source of an average existence or the seed of your superhuman ability.

The choice is yours.

"Mind is the Master Power that moulds and makes,
And Man is Mind, and evermore he takes
The tool of Thought, and, shaping what he wills,
Brings forth a thousand joys, or a thousand ills:
He thinks in secret, and it comes to pass:
Environment is but his looking-glass." - James Allen

6
DEFINING SUCCESS

The clarity with which we define something determines its usefulness. "- Tony Blauer

You already know that I am a fan of clear definitions. The quote above has made a huge impact on how I learn, how I make progress and how I teach and communicate with others.

You will see the recurring theme throughout the rest of this book. The more clearly we can define our thoughts, feelings, words and actions, the better they will serve us. The more clearly we can describe the end result we desire, the more likely we are to arrive there and the less problems we will have along the way.

We all want success. But what does that mean exactly? A strong argument could be made that it is very much up to the individual to define it. I can get behind that. I also know that if you don't define it, then you won't know what it means.

Think of someone who, in your opinion, is very successful. One name that immediately comes to mind for me is Arnold Schwarzenegger. His story is truly remarkable, beginning as a poor farm boy in a tiny village in Austria and rising to the very top of the sport of bodybuilding, becoming one of the biggest movie stars in history and then becoming governor of California. Whether you like him, enjoy his movies or share his political views doesn't matter, you have to agree that he has become very successful in many areas. Not the least of which is introducing some snappy one liners into pop culture.

"The mind will always fail first, not the body. The secret is to make your mind work for you, not against you." ~Arnold Schwarzenegger

Who do you think of when you think of extreme success? It doesn't have to be a public figure. It could be someone that you know personally. What does the person you chose have in common with Arnold? Is your choice an expert or champion at something? Famous? Wealthy? Do they have the ability to inspire others?

Now, let's look at the lives, actions and habits of the "average" person. They wake up. They go to work at a job that they may not love or may even hate, but it pays the bills. They come home, spend some "quality time" with family sitting around the TV, maybe fool around on the internet and social media, go to bed so that they can wake up the next day and repeat the cycle. I could go on and on, but you get the idea.

This represents a vast majority of the people. People who really have no idea why they are doing what they are doing, other than "that's what you do. You go to work, you earn some money so that you can pay your bills. That's what everyone does." But is doing what everyone else does because everyone else does it the best way to go? Does it make one fulfilled? Happy? Successful?

Most of us would respond with "NO". So, why then, do so many people take this path?

I believe it is because we are taught from a very early age to be "realistic", to behave well and to not cause any trouble. Another way to put it is that we are taught to *conform*. It feels safe to conform. To do as we are told. To avoid risk. It requires little courage or daring. Yet conformity is the very thing that crushes the spirit of those who might soar.

"The opposite of courage in our society is not cowardice, it is conformity". Rollo May

If we choose to follow the crowd, to fit in, then we are choosing to be average, not superhuman. We also choose to have the results that are average.

Let's go back to the definition of success.

How many of us have ever sat down and deliberately decided on a definition of success?

Years ago, I was working a 40+ hour a week job that I hated and it was taking a toll on me. I decided to enroll in a school to become a licensed massage therapist. This eventually led me into the strength and fitness business and becoming a strongman, although I didn't have a clue at the time that any of that was in my future.

While in massage school, I was in a business class and didn't realize that my entire life was about to be affected by a single question on an assignment.

That question:

"What would your life look like if you were successful?"

This lead to an open discussion in the class of everyone sharing their idea of the answer. After much deliberation and discussion I came to realize my answer.

I already WAS successful.

I knew that I wasn't fulfilled in what I was doing at the other job. I had chosen a new career path and I was there in a class, learning about this chosen profession. I was taking steps toward changing my life into the life I wanted. I knew where I was headed and I had a plan to get there.

Later on, this concept was crystallized into the definition of success that I still use. It comes from the personal development pioneer, Earl Nightingale:

Success is the Progressive Realization of a Worthy Ideal.

So, who is successful? Anyone who is doing what they deliberately decided to do and doing it well.

If you have set a goal for yourself, something that has meaning for you and are actively taking measures to accomplish that goal, then you are ALREADY successful. You don't have to accomplish everything that you want in order to achieve success. In fact, the moment you decide on a goal and begin taking action toward it, you create success, because you actively and intentionally take a small step toward the Realization of your own Worthy Ideal.

Success comes not from doing certain things, but from doing them in a certain way. In the next few pages, you'll find out exactly what that certain way is and how to apply it to your own Success.

7
TOWARD A DEEPER UNDERSTANDING

Let's bring some clarity to this. Let's take the above definition and scrutinize it a little more closely. In order to fully grasp the message, we will take a look at each word, beginning with the Ideal, and then see with greater clarity the sum of all the words.

PROGRESSIVE- *Going forward or onward; passing successively from one member of a series to the next; proceeding step by step.*

Progress is continually moving in the direction of the objective. This doesn't always mean in a straight line. Sometimes progress doesn't appear as progress. Sometimes it may look as if you are sidetracked or even moving in the opposite direction. However, if you keep the ideal fixed in your mind continuously and take actions toward it, you will still be progressing. My good friend and fellow strongman Adam Glass has described progress as "Moving forward in any direction."

Have you ever had your GPS re-route you because of traffic? Sometimes it will take you in a direction that seems to have nothing to do with the destination. You are OK with that because you know that in this case, the indirect route is actually the one with the least obstacles. Sometimes the longer road is the better path.

Two things are necessary in order to continually be progressing toward our worthy ideal.

1. Thought: We must hold it in our mind most of the time. Remember, we become what we think about. If we continually think of our worthy ideal, ways to bring it into being, imagining that we have already attained it and experiencing the emotions that are associated with succeeding, then we are certain to arrive there.

2. Action: We must perform activities that are in harmony with the desired outcome of the ideal. Thinking alone will not get us where we want to go. Once we have the thought firmly implanted, we must take action on a daily basis that is in harmony with that thought. Do this long enough and you are guaranteed success.

REALIZATION - *the making or being made real of something imagined or planned.*

If we use both words together, we begin to describe movement. To Progressively Realize something means to bring it from thought into reality. What was once imagined becomes actualized in the physical world.

ALL things began first as an idea in someone's imagination.

Realization is to take whatever is in our thoughts and make it into something that exists in this physical reality. If you think about it, the light bulb, the laptop computer, the automobile, the airplane; none of that stuff existed in physical reality 150 years ago, but the natural laws that govern the planet we live on haven't changed. So the potential for all of those things has always been there, which is kind of a crazy thing to think about.

If we knew how a hundred years ago, we could have made the internet and the iPhone. But we didn't know how and it took a progressive series of steps, the awareness of natural laws, the understanding of how to use resources and how to think in order to get us to where we are now. This is beginning to get into what a superhuman mind truly is; a creative expression of ourselves.

WORTHY - *having adequate or great merit, character, or value:*

At this point you may be thinking that you must be worthy of whatever ideal you are seeking to accomplish. Are you up to the task? Are you good enough? Are you smart enough? Talented enough? Do you have what it takes to represent this ideal to it's full potential and realization?

That makes sense, it sounds a lot like setting a goal and going after it. And on a certain level it is. You may find yourself asking: "Am I worthy of the goals that I have? Am I good enough to achieve them?" I think a lot of us are like that. I have had those thoughts before and I can certainly see why you might think that. But I want to offer another point of view, a different way to consider it. A better question to ask is: "Is this goal worthy of my energy, my attention and my dedicating my life to accomplishing it?"

Put another way: Is the Ideal worthy of you?

That's right. Is IT worthy of YOU??

Is it something that has enough merit and enough value that you are willing to devote your time, your attention and your energy toward it? You are important. You are a magnificent creation. Does the Ideal deserve your attention, energy and intent? Is the ideal worthy of you?

When I had that shift in my thinking it opened up a lot of new possibilities for me. Super human possibilities. For example, when it came time to get started writing this book. "Am I good enough to write about this?" Or "is this a good enough subject matter for me to write about?" Those are two completely different ways of looking at it.

Whether you are good enough or not should never be a question. All of us are born with the same potential and the same promise as the greatest figures in history. We were all born a completely blank slate with infinite possibility. We all have that potential in us.

When I decided to write this book, my question for myself was: "Is this worthy of me? Is talking and writing about this subject, doing feats of strength, teaching other people how to make their lives better. Is that worthy of my time and energy?" I, of course, decided that it was or else you wouldn't be reading this. The worthy doesn't have to do with the individual. It has to do with the Ideal.

Is it good enough for you to do? If it's not then move on to something else that is.

IDEAL - *an ultimate object or aim of endeavor, especially one of high or noble character.*

The Ideal is the central thing. Without it, none of the rest of the definition matters, indeed not much matters at all without an Ideal. You might have heard it called by other names. Passion. Purpose. Vision. Dream. Goal. These are all great terms. They all describe various aspects of the Ideal. This the End Game for you.

I have heard it put another way: an Ideal is an Idea that you have fallen in love with. I like that one a lot.

Here is where we find the essence of your superhuman self.

If you have a clear vision of your Ideal and you hold it in your mind's eye consistently and continuously, you will automatically move toward it. The Ideal, the destination, the vision is the most important thing. Without it, you have no idea where you are going. When you imprint it into your mind, you will know. You may not know how, but that doesn't matter. If the Ideal is held in the mind and you get emotionally involved with it then the way will make itself known.

When you hold this ideal in your mind, this vision will inspire you to act in a way that is in line with it's fulfillment. Without the ideal, even if you are taking action, you are like a hamster on a wheel. The ideal, the vision, is what directs your actions.

"He who cherishes a beautiful vision, a lofty ideal in his heart, will one day realize it." James Allen, *As a Man Thinketh,*

Your worthy ideal is loaded with great value. It is something that stirs your heart and inspires you to move toward a better version of yourself, a fuller expression of who you are. It is loaded with great value. It will inspire you to continue, no matter what obstacle may arise.

It is the discovery and development of your unique super powers. I keep tossing out that term, but what does it really mean?

Super is a Latin adjective meaning above, high quality, large or powerful.

Power refers to mental or moral efficacy or physical might. The Middle English origin goes back to the Anglo-Norman French word *poeir*, from an alteration of Latin *posse* 'be able.' It is also related to the latin root *pote* which is where we get the word "potential".

Your *super power* then, is something that enables you to express your potential in a way that is large, powerful and shows high quality,

No one can even begin to predict with any accuracy the potential that each of us has. I can tell you that very few of us ever have the courage to travel that road that leads us toward it. Those that do wind up forever altering the landscape of the world around them.

The Wright brothers.

Edison.

Steve Jobs.

Oprah.

Arnold.

Super powers are not brought about by radioactive spiders or being exposed to gamma rays. The well that they spring from is our ability to think and imagine. Planes, iPhone, etc were all once just thoughts in the imaginations of the men that had the drive to progressively realize them.

Thought is the master power, imagination is the laboratory and habit is the fuel.

"There is no such thing as a little man. Think that you are strong and you are....." the Mighty Atom.

8

THOUGHT

"A man is literally what he thinks, his character being the complete sum of all his thoughts." - James Allen, As a Man Thinketh

All throughout history, wise men, philosophers, etc, have disagreed on just about everything, except for this truth that we keep coming back to:

We become what we think about.

You already know that I was first introduced to this concept when reading *Think and Grow Rich* and that it was the central idea of the movie *The Secret* a few years ago. That movie got a fair amount of backlash from some folks because it "didn't work" but if you look at the behavior and mindset of the people complaining, you'll see that it worked absolutely. The negative result that was produced was exactly in harmony with the dominant thoughts of doubt, lack and negativity of the thinker. They may not have gotten what they wanted, but they got what they expected.

The person who sets their mind on a gigantic goal will achieve it.

The person who sets their mind on an average goal will achieve it.

The person consumed by thoughts of worry, doubt, guilt and fear will live a life of worry, doubt, guilt and fear.

The person who has no goal? They will achieve that. As the saying goes, if you don't have a 5 year goal for yourself, then you are already there.......

If you plant tomatoes in a garden, you grow tomatoes. If you plant flowers, you grow flowers. In either case, would you expect to grow apples? Of course not. We know that the land will return only that which is planted. At the same time, the garden will do far better is it is kept, if the weeds are removed and the plants are watered and cared for.

The mind is like the soil, only far more fertile. Whatever thoughts we plant will bear fruit that is in alignment with those thoughts. If we plant thoughts of success, advancement, happiness, health and prosperity in our mind, those are the fruits we enjoy. If we plant thoughts of failure, depression, sickness, confusion, and poverty, then that is what we reap. If we don't plant anything, then whatever happens to land there from the outside world will take root and grow, like weeds.

Just as the earth doesn't care what is planted, neither does our mind. We are creative beings. Everything around us is a product of this.

Many of us are operating with inherited belief systems that do not serve us. These belief systems have created the results that we are currently experiencing and often we do not like or want those results. It is very easy to become so focused on the thing that we don't like or don't want that we never clearly define the thing that we DO want.

In school we are taught to read, do math, to memorize a bunch of stuff. But as far as I know there is not a single class on how to think creatively.

Our thoughts are creative in nature. Everything around us began as a thought, an idea. The building you are in was first a set of blueprints. The car, the computer, the airplane, the sidewalk, the internet.....everything began as an idea....a THOUGHT in someone's mind.

Also, bear in mind that nothing was ever built by thinking of what ISN'T wanted. It always comes from what IS desired.

HABITS

Our habits determine our results. Our mind, specifically our subconscious mind, determines our habits. Our subconscious acts as a cybernetic mechanism. What does that mean exactly?

Cybernetics refers to a self-regulating system which typically works through error correction. Your air conditioner maintains temperature by using a cybernetic device, what we call a thermostat. You set a thermostat to a desired temperature, say 70 degrees F. If the temperature in the house rises above 70, the thermostat senses it and turns on the AC. When the interior reaches the correct temperature, the thermostat turns it off. The temperature you set is the "goal". The AC is a "goal-seeking" system that works to automatically regulate itself by sensing the temperature gap between the goal and the actual temperature. It then goes to work and gets back on track by going in the opposite direction from the "error".

Most of the cybernetic systems in your body are completely automatic, but we also have learned behaviors or skills that are cybernetic systems, like walking and riding a bicycle. The trick in leaning how to ride a bicycle is making the error correction automatic. The key to breaking old habits is programming our subconscious mind to make new habits automatic.

Dr. Maxwell Maltz, author of the book *Psycho-Cybernetics,* viewed the subconscious mind as our goal-seeking mechanism. Maltz was a plastic surgeon who observed that his patients often suffered from self-image problems and that corrective surgery did not always result in correction of the "mutilated self-image".

He found that the subconscious mind acted like a cybernetic mechanism depending upon the goal. When the subconscious mind is given a "success goal" it acts like a "success mechanism". When given a negative goal it will act as a "failure mechanism".

The subconscious mind acts as a storage center, like your computers hard drive. Every impulse of thought, from any of the five senses is received and recorded, regardless of the nature of the thought. These thoughts link together to form paradigms and belief systems, which in turn are expressed by the body as habit and behavior, much like your operating system.

What we do automatically and habitually is often referred to as unconscious, in that we do not give conscious thought to it. As babies and children, much of our belief system is programmed into us by our environment: parents, relatives, media, etc. Later in life these beliefs systems…the inherited thought patterns of those who were around us at an early age….guide us and give us results. If we stray very far from our paradigm, our subconscious corrects the error and pulls us back "on course" to our imbedded belief system, just like the thermostat regulating the temperature of the room.

Did you ever set a goal for yourself, kick major ass in the direction of it's accomplishment and then do something that moved you in the opposite direction, for no apparent reason? I know I have. I believe we all have at one time or another.

You know what to do. You KNOW BETTER than to do something, but you do it anyway. And oddly, you cannot explain WHY you chose to do it. I'll tell you why this happens: The auto-pilot of the subconscious isn't in agreement with the goal, so you set yourself up to fail, to conform with the image you have of yourself.

A classic example of this is the story we hear every so often of the poor person who wins the lottery and then within a couple of years is in a worse position than they were before winning. Even though they won the money, their mind still sees them as being "poor" and try as they might, unless that poor image is reprogrammed it ain't gonna match up to being wealthy. They will correct themselves back to what they believe that they are: poor.

The good news is that if you are not satisfied with your results, you can use your conscious mind to actively and deliberately reprogram your subconscious mind to become exactly who and what you want to be.

How do you do that? The upcoming exercises deal with this in detail, but the short answer is to hold in your conscious mind a clear and detailed picture of yourself having already achieved your goal, and this is best done in a relaxed and happy emotional state, grateful for the thing that you have accomplished.

Yes, I am telling you to be thankful for the thing you want to accomplish, before you accomplish it, so that you may accomplish it.

If you desire something and can paint a clear and detailed picture of it in your mind, you can create whatever you desire in your life.

"Whether you believe that you can or you believe you cannot, either way you are correct." - Henry Ford

Success and failure are born from the same thought energy. It takes equal amount of thought energy to either be the person who looks at a car and thinks "I can't afford to buy that car" or to be the person who looks at the car dealership and thinks "I'm going to buy this car dealership." We all have these mental faculties. The two people in those two situations have the same faculties. It's a matter of how they're being applied.

"I can't do that." versus "How can I do that?" It is all the same energy. It's just a matter of how the energy is directed. Nothing is in inherently good or bad about the energy. It is all a matter of how you direct it.

I have a trick question for you. Electricity - is it good or is it bad?

If you want to light your house and cook your food, use your computer and drive your car, then electricity is good.

I'm a fan of electricity but if I take a fork and stick it in a wall socket then the electricity is not so good for me, right? It is the same energy, and I can either use it to my advantage or to my detriment. Thought energy works the same way.

This thought energy is ultimately controlled by our hidden self-image. That self-image controls our mind, just as certainly as our mind controls our breathing. The primary cause for success or failure in all of us is the ability to direct this thought energy.

Whether or not you want to admit it, your self-image controls everything you do. We all have a picture in our mind of who we are, what we are and what kind of person we are. It drives everything that we do. How successful you are in any undertaking will never be greater than the image you have of yourself.

We've all been around (and some of us have actually been) the person who decides that they're going to join the gym and lose 30lbs, get healthy and take control of that aspect of their lives.

They tighten up their diet, hit the gym and lose 30lbs. Six months later they are 40lbs heavier than before they started. They gained it all back, plus interest. They did the work, got the result and then they undid it and went back to where they came from. Why is that? Just like our poor-minded lotto winner, it is because of the self -image.

The self-image corrected them back to the person they think they are. The self-image regulates everything unconsciously. It determines how we act. It significantly affects our success.

Our self-image was, for the most part, formed from past experiences. We are the product of someone else's habitual way of thinking. When we are born we don't have the ability to create our own self-image. We are just absorbing from our environment and our parents, from our friends and teachers at school, from our religious leaders, from the media and TV, radio, internet, whatever. We are absorbing all this information and we put it together and we look at the circumstances and we look at the information and we find things that match up and we form our self -image based on that.

We all have seen pictures of emaciated girls with eating disorders that are just skin and bones and they still think they're fat. They look in the mirror and don't see what the external is; they see the internal image of an overweight girl.

Here is the good news: Your self-image is not permanent. It is malleable and it can be changed, exactly the same way it was formed: through repetition. But in this case it will be the repetition of thoughts that you originate and feed it. You have complete control over this.

Nothing and no one can prevent you from improving your self image.

If you don't like the results that you're getting, if you don't like the way your life is, if you don't like the way that you are and you know that it is driven by your self-image, then you can change your self-image. From whatever it is into a superhuman version of what you want it to be. You can find your own superpower, the worthy ideal to change your self-image and become that person.

Arnold Schwarzenegger, when he was a poor boy in the Army, saw himself as a world champion bodybuilder. He saw himself as a highly paid movie actor. Very early on he established that vision. He held it in his mind and ultimately it came to physical realization.

There are people who continually struggle to improve, trying to change the end result. Those results are determined by their actions and those actions are being driven by their self image. They have not yet come to understand that the results are a direct reflection of their self image.

But how do you do it? Keep reading……

9
THE PROCESS

As you move toward your superhuman success, you will be using a three stage process.

1. Inspiration
2. Imagination
3. Action

This is a step by step process that will result in the accomplishment of whatever you decide to pursue.

Don't be fooled by the seeming simplicity of it. This formula has worked countless times for countless people pursuing countless goals. Some of them did so without understanding the process, you may have even done it yourself. But being unaware of the process doesn't mean that the process want being used.

INSPIRATION

Believe it is possible.

Earlier I told you how inspired I became as a little kid seeing Lou Ferrigno on TV. This was my inspiration, that spark of an idea that set the whole thing in motion. Inspiration is the stirring in your soul that says "I want to be more than I am… I want to have more… I want to do more!" What you are really saying is "I want to be super human".

This inspiration is in all of us. We do not want to be stuck in the same spot. We all want to do or be or have something better than we are experiencing right now. That often gets squashed from the outside before we even get started because we are told we "should be happy with what we have".

We may feel guilty about it because we're taught that it is greedy to want more.

We may feel inadequate because our grand fantasies as children were often met with "we can't afford it" or "you'll never be able to do that".

You can be happy with what you have, but you do not have to be content with it. Those are two different things. I'm so incredibly happy and grateful for everything in my life and I'm also excited about the possibility and the promise of better things, more exciting experiences and all of the expansion that is occurring on a day to day basis. It is a healthy dissatisfaction.

It all starts with that spark of possibility, that inspiration.

When I saw Lou Ferrigno for the fist time dressed as the Hulk and realized that it was not just a cartoon or comic book thing, that was not just made up, it became real. It became possible that there really were people that are big and strong. That was when it stopped being just a sheer fantasy that floated around my mind and became something that was possible to do. The shift in my perception was immediate and permanent. My level of awareness had risen.

Years later when I first read about The Mighty Atom and how he would bite nails in half, the same thing happened. There was a short time of wonder and thinking "How can that even be possible?" Then my awareness shifted again toward the superhuman. I never met the Mighty Atom, he died when I was a child, but I have met many people who did, people who knew him and witnessed some of these incredible things first hand. I have handled pieces of steel he bent. They are real. It wasn't a trick, it was a deeper level of awareness of his own potential and power.

I have seen some pretty fantastic things since then from other strongmen as well.

Once you believe it's possible, the next step, if you truly want to move in that direction, is to start looking at people who are already doing the thing that you want to do and pick out the things that you like about their approach to it.

When I first started training to become a strongman, I learned a lot from Dennis Rogers about the fundamentals and the classic feats of strength. Things like bending spikes and horse shoes and tearing decks of cards. I became interested in

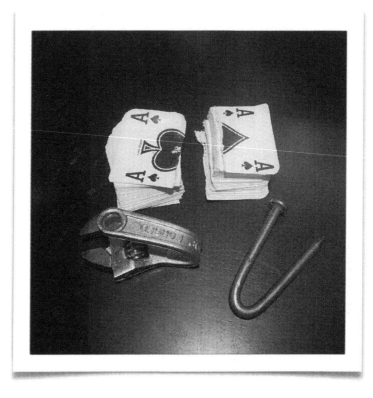

leverage lifting sledgehammers. Dennis doesn't do much leverage lifting but his mentor, Slim The Hammer Man does.

I told Dennis I was interested in leverage lifting and he told me to study Slim. So I started watching video of Slim. I started emulating his technique in order to understand how he was doing it. I had to understand how I could do what he does first and only then could I adapt it and make it my own. Every leverage lift that I do is an homage to Slim The Hammer Man, for sure.

Eventually I had the opportunity to perform a hammer lift in front of Slim, with one of his hammers. He looked at me suspiciously and asked "Who showed you how to do that?"

I grinned "You did, Slim." He then showed me some of the subtle things that I hadn't noticed which immediately resulted in a new all-time best lift for me.

This happens all the time with musicians. You may not know this about me, but I love me some Lady Gaga. Absolutely love her. Prior to Lady Gaga, I grew up in the 80's listening to Madonna. So, of course I like Lady Gaga.

If you take Madonna and David Bowie and put them in the Brundlefly teleporter thingie, then Lady Gaga comes out the other side. Her influences are obvious and yet she is uniquely herself. She has taken her influences, internalized them and created a new thing, an expression of who she is.

Look at Stevie Ray Vaughn and then compare that to Albert King and Jimi Hendrix. It is the same kind of development.

Arnold Schwarzenegger emulated Reg Park. He took everything Reg Park did and did it times ten! This is how successful people operate. They choose bits and pieces of mentors and influences and they craft it together in a way that makes it all their own.

As you do this, you are reinforcing the fact that your goal is not only possible, but you are starting to believe it is possible for YOU. In the next exercise you will consciously and deliberately choose the attributes of your influences.

EXERCISE:

Make a list of at least 7 successful people who exhibit qualities that you admire and would like to emulate. From this you will begin to build a model of the superhuman you.

1. _____
2. _____
3. _____
4. _____
5. _____
6. _____
7. _____

Now that you have your list, consider what it is about them that inspires you. Choose aspects from each of them.

How do they talk? How do they dress? How do they interact with others? Can you begin to imagine yourself in their position?

For each of the people you listed, write out one or two qualities about them that inspire you.

1. _____
   _____
   _____

2. _____
   _____
   _____

3. _____
   _____
   _____

4. _____
   _____
   _____

5. _____
   _____
   _____

6. _____
   _____
   _____

7. _____
   _____
   _____

IMAGINATION

"Imagination is the most marvelous, miraculous, inconceivable, powerful force that the world has ever known."
— *Napoleon Hill*

"Imagination is more important than knowledge, for knowledge is limited to all we now know and understand, while imagination embraces the entire world, and all there ever will be to know and understand."
— *Albert Einstein*

Dream BIG

We all have that voice in our head, you know the one. It is the voice that says "wouldn't it be cool if....". Learn to listen to that voice. Learn to trust it. It is the sound of your higher self seeking full expression of your super powerful self.

If inspiration means to believe it is possible, then imagination means to believe it is possible.......for YOU.

When he commissioned Napoleon Hill to spend 20 years documenting his philosophy for success, Andrew Carnegie also issued a challenge to Hill. At the time Hill deemed it impossible. But having given his word to Carnegie, he pursued it anyway. He later recounted the story in his writings. I got this story from Bob Proctor's website, written by Hill in his own words:

Carnegie said, "I want you to write very slowly and I want you to underscore every word that I speak now. And here's the message that I want you to repeat to yourself, at least twice a day - once just before you go to bed at night and once just after you get up. Looking at yourself in a mirror...you're talking to Napoleon Hill now, mind you. And here's what you say to him: 'Andrew Carnegie, I'm not only going to equal your achievements in life, but I'm going to challenge you at the post and pass you at the grandstand.'

And I threw my pencil down and I said, "Now, Mr. Carnegie, let's be realistic. You know very well I'm not going to be able to do that!" At that time, Mr. Carnegie was rated as a billionaire - probably the first and maybe the only billionaire this country has ever created as far as I know. He said, "Why, of course, I know you're not going to be able to do that, unless and until you believe it! But if you believe it, you will." He said, "Let me ask you to do this. Try it out for 30 days. Will you do that?" I said, "Yes, that's a reasonable request, I certainly will."

But I had the fingers on both hands crossed. I knew dog-gone well it wouldn't work. The idea of a youngster, in his early 20's, promising to equal and outdo the achievements of a man who had reached the stage of a billionaire. Why, it was so ridiculous, it wasn't even funny. It even scared me. I thought Mr. Carnegie had lost his mind. I came very near to walking out on him. It was just something that was too good to be true. But I promised, and when I got back to Washington - my brother and I had an apartment - and I went to look over this formula, I didn't want my brother to know what a big fool I had made of myself, because I had some news to break to him that was not going to be good anyway. I had agreed to pay the expenses of the two of us through school and I was going to have to tell him that I was dropping out and that he would have to earn his own way.

I went into the bathroom and I closed the door real tight, and I got real close up to the glass and almost whispered this formula. As I turned around - in my mind's eye - I saw the real Napoleon Hill standing there, and I said, "You darn liar, you know very well you're not going to be able to do that." Only 'darn' was not the word I used. It was a much more definite and stronger word. I felt like a fool, like a thief, going through a thing like that - a farce. And that's just what it seemed like. But I said, "Well, after all, you promised Mr. Carnegie, go ahead and try it."

For the first week - just about the first week - I had the attitude or feeling like I was doing something foolish. Then all of a sudden, about the beginning of the second week, something inside of me said, "Why don't you change your mental attitude about this? Do you realize that Andrew Carnegie is the richest man in the world; that he is known all over the world as the best picker of men in the world; and if he chose you, to do a job like this, he must have found something in you that you didn't know was there. Why don't you change your mental attitude?"

I started to change my mental attitude. If I hadn't have done so, I wouldn't be talking to you today, and I wouldn't be talking to millions of people in this and other countries of the free world through my books, if I hadn't changed my mental attitude and become positive instead of negative.

I started to repeat this in earnest, and by the end of the month, I not only believed I'd catch up with Mr. Carnegie, but I KNEW that I would excel that man. And believe you me, when I tell you that I have long since achieved that objective. I'll tell you why I've achieved it. Mr. Carnegie made not over

20 or 25 millionaires at the most. The millionaires that I have had the privilege of making, they're legion - they're all over the world."

While Napoleon Hill never accumulated the monetary fortune of Carnegie, if we consider the effects of his messages of inspiration, which continue to ripple out into the universe to this day, then Hill absolutely passed him at the grandstand. Hill's enormous influence has helped millions of people find themselves, believe in themselves and realize their dreams. That was his superhuman power.

Carnegie saw something in Hill, something that Hill himself could not see. Hill realized a dream that he initially deemed impossible. He did this by using his imagination to construct a vision of a superhuman version of himself.

In Think and Grow Rich, Hill states that there are actually two types of imagination.

First, there is the synthetic imagination. This where we take existing ideas and concepts and rearrange them into something new.

Think of a car. An image of a car comes to mind. Now think of a pickup truck. Make the truck blue in your mind. Now change it's color to red. See how that works? You used existing ideas of both cars, trucks and colors, then combined them to create a new image.

Then there is creative imagination. When new ideas come into our minds and we create something that literally wasn't there before. Have you ever had a thought or an idea for some new product, and then within a few months someone else has brought that product to market? This is the creative imagination at work.

They work in concert with each other, and in order to utilize them we must exercise both of them. Little kids use their imagination all the time. When I was a boy, my bike could be a space ship that I was in, hurtling through some distant galaxy or a dinosaur that I was riding across a prehistoric landscape. Sticks became swords or magic wands. We all did this kind of thing. We all still have that ability to imagine in our minds, even if we allowed it to atrophy from lack of use.

It is also important to Dream BIG; if you just say: "uh....I dunno.... I kinda want to make a little bit more money next year, I guess" or "It might be nice to lose a little weight" or "I wouldn't mind adding a few pounds to my bench press"; That's not a big dream. It is not a worthy ideal. It is not super human.

Joe Vitale says that a goal or a dream should excite you a lot and scare you a little. So if you're not a little bit scared by it, it's not big enough. If someone else has done it then certainly you should be able to do it. Look at Richard Branson, not just his money, but look at the adventure that he lives in his life. He has an idea and he executes it. I suspect he would still be living some kind of adventure even if he didn't have the money. I think the money is a symptom of his enthusiasm for life, I don't think it's the driving cause of it. So dream BIG.

Whatever your dream is; amplify it, multiply it times ten. Make it bigger than you think is possible and then believe that it is possible for you to do it. You may be like Hill, unable to believe it at first but through repetition of focusing your attention on this dream, this worthy ideal, you come to believe that it is possible.

Once you have the idea in your mind, take some time to sit down and construct on paper in great detail what the vision looks like.

Often we describe success in terms of a few things that we like or want and a lot of things that we DON'T want. I have an exercise that I do and that I recommend to people when they are feeling stuck thinking of what they don't want and are having trouble figuring out what they DO want.

This exercise will bring clarity to what you actually DO want and get you moving in the direction you want to go.

HOW TO DECIDE WHAT YOU WANT

I got this exercise from Bob Proctor. I have personalized it a bit and encourage you to do the same. The purpose here is to decide exactly what you really want.

All to often we express our desires in terms of what we don't want....

I don't want to be so stressed out.
I don't want to be broke.
I don't want to worry about money.
I don't want to be fat.
I don't want to feel this way.

You get the idea. The problem here is that by declaring what we don't want, we are focusing on the very thing we don't want. Want proof? Right now, whatever you do do NOT think about big pink elephants. Seriously, don't do it. Stop thinking of that elephant.

The more you "try" to stop, the less success you had, right? Now, think of your kitchen, specifically the refrigerator door. Picture yourself standing in front of it, opening it up and taking out a bottle of water. See and feel yourself taking the top off and having a sip. Feel the coolness of it on your lips, taste it as you swallow it and feel the coolness in your throat. Got it? Good. You forgot all about that elephant, didn't you?

See how that works? In order to stop thinking of one thing, I gave you something different to focus on. I asked you to involve more of your senses and imagination as well, to make it more real, more powerful.

We are gonna do the same thing on a more serious and personal scale now. I have included sheets marked for this exercise starting on page 81, but you can easily do it with any kind of paper. I strongly recommend that you do all the writing by hand, rather than typing it into a document on your computer. Using a pen or pencil will get you more personally involved in the process.

1. Across the top of one sheet of paper, write NEGATIVE, just like the example sheet. On the other one write POSITIVE.

2. On the NEGATIVE sheet:
Write down the thing that you don't want or the stuff about yourself that you don't like. Something that you want to change, something like the "I don't want..." list above. The thing that is blocking you from opening up your superhuman mind and discovering and developing your superpower. I bend steel and talk about the mind, but your superpower might be doing amazing things with animals or homeless people. Think of something that drives you, inspires you and makes you feel superhuman.

Think of all the reasons that you CAN'T do it. These can be things that someone else told you or things that you have told yourself.

As you think of these things, write them down. Write down all the things that you don't like. Just take this terrible, ugly thing that makes you cry that you don't want anybody to know about and write it out. Feel all the emotions that go along with it as much as you can in this written description on this piece of paper.

Write out in great detail all the things about it you don't want. With regards to your body it might be how you look, feel, health concerns, etc. If it's money, write about how you worry and get stressed. In whatever way you are limited, physically, emotionally, whatever...write out in details how you feel when you are feeling your worst...and as you write, FEEL those things fully. You may cry. You may get angry or feel shame....that's OK. Keep writing, it's for a good reason.

3. On the POSITIVE sheet:
On the first line write "I am so happy and grateful now that ...."

Now, when you get done blowing your nose and feeling terrible about life, look over all the stuff on the first page, go sentence by sentence through your negative description and REWRITE IT so that it is the exact 180 degree opposite of what you described.

For example if you wrote down on your piece of paper "I don't want to be broke anymore" or "I hate being broke" on the other piece of paper write down " I love that I have all the money that I need." If you described feeling distress from lack of money, write about how relaxed and happy you feel knowing that you have more than enough to buy the things you want and need.

If you wrote down "I hate being fat" or "I don't want to be weak", write down the opposite of that: "I love that I am lean" and "I am happy that I am strong." If you described feeling embarrassed in a bathing suit, write about how

awesome you feel being lean. You get the idea. In great detail describe how amazing and awesome and happy you feel.
There are two critical factors that you must include:

1. Really FEEL it as you write it.

2. Write it in the PRESENT TENSE.

Your subconscious mind cannot make a distinction between what is real and what is imagined. By making it present tense, your subconscious will begin immediately to find a way to make it exist in the present reality.

4. Once you've written out the positive description, take the first piece of paper, the NEGATIVE sheet and set fire to it. Burn it and release it into the universe forever. I mean literally set fire to it and let it go and let the ashes fly. This is symbolically releasing the old habit and the first action step in freeing yourself from the old thought pattern.

5. Take the POSITIVE sheet and rewrite it by hand first thing every morning, feel the feelings associated, in the PRESENT tense. Feel the love and forgiveness you have for yourself. At least 3 more times every day, read the description aloud, with one of those times being right before bed.

Rewrite it again the next morning and repeat the affirmation throughout the day until it becomes habitual. Do this every single day, for 90 days. You may alter it as your vision becomes more and more clear. As you rewrite it and read it, use you imagination to experience what it is like to have already accomplished the goal. Mix all that emotion with it and feel it as if it has actually happened.

Remember that the subconscious mind cannot differentiate between that which is imagined and that which is real. Because of this, you will write out your goal in great detail AND in the present tense.

Do not say "I want to" or "I will" but rather "I AM".

To make it even more effective, we include gratitude in the description. From Bob Proctor I learned the value of beginning the statement with "I am so happy and grateful now that I am….". Being grateful keeps you in a mindset that focuses on what you want. If you can be thankful for something before it has been realized, then you are truly expressing your super human mind. The goal is accomplished in your mind first. Then it manifests physically.

If you want, you can rewrite it 10 to 20 times a day every day for three months. You will be amazed at how much your attention, your awareness and the fact that you're focusing on what you actually want in great detail will begin to attract those things into your life.

NEGATIVE

_____

_____

_____

_____

_____

_____

_____

_____

_____

_____

_____

_____

_____

_____

_____

_____

_____

_____

_____

_____

_____

_____

_____

_____

_____

_____

_____

_____

_____

POSITIVE

CONSTRUCTING YOUR SUPERHUMAN VISION

As your ability to use your imagination to create your future continues to develop, you will be able to write out goals and ideals more and more easily, using your creative power. Here is a quick story about how to create a vision and bring it into the physical.

In 2013, I decided that I wanted to certify on the IronMind Red Nail. The Red Nail is a piece of cold rolled steel that is 7 inches long and 5/16 of an inch thick. I won't bore you with the details, but to certify on it, it must be bent under certain very specific conditions, including a one-minute time limit. This must be done in front of an impartial referee.

Getting my name on the list was a worthy ideal for me because some of the most respected steel benders in the world have done it. I constructed a vision of myself completing this feat that was so detailed that I could feel the texture of the wraps and smell the chalk.

Every day, in addition to specific training for it, I would imagine bending the Red Nail. I had a small group of people watching in addition to my referee. I did not construct their faces, but I did see them, sitting in a semi-circle in my gym. I could feel their energy and encouragement. I could hear them applaud and congratulate me after I bent the nail. My best time for bending it in practice was about 40 seconds. In my vision the nail bent like a stick of chewing gum and I completed it in 20 seconds.

Events were set in motion and when the day finally came, it was in my gym at the beginning of the Oldetime Strongman

University workshop with Dennis Rogers. I was hosting the workshop and assisting with the teaching.

My referee, Tim Dial, arrived. We talked a bit and he presented me with the nail that I would be using for my certification.

Wrapping and chalking the nail, taking position in front of the attendees (which included my chi kung and meditation teacher James Alexander, fellow strongman Mike the Machine Bruce and of course, Dennis Rogers) and completing the bend were all exactly as it was in my vision.

The only difference was the time it took to complete:

16 seconds.

I had created a better reality than my vision!

To construct your superhuman vision statement, you will take the list of qualities you made in the Influences exercise on page 69 and the description of your desire from the Positive paper exercise on page 82 and combine them together into a vision statement. This superhuman image will be the basis you use to reprogram your mind for superhuman success.

For your next exercise, write it out with great detail and in the present tense.

Begin with "I am so happy and grateful now that I am...." and then fill out the rest of the description.

Red Nail = Dead Nail

SUPER HUMAN VISION STATEMENT

_____

_____

_____

_____

_____

_____

_____

_____

_____

_____

_____

_____

_____

_____

_____

_____

_____

_____

_____

_____

_____

_____

_____

_____

_____

_____

_____

_____

ACTION

"Knowing is not enough; we must apply. Willing is not enough; we must do."- Johann Wolfgang Von Goethe

It is not enough to think about your dream. It is not enough to talk about it. In order to fulfill your worthy ideal, you must apply action.

If I had only imagined bending a Red Nail but never done the physical training, I would still be imagining with no physical result. The good news is that by writing it out, you have already taken the first action towards it and you are already gathering momentum!

Now we come to a very important element. Consistency. We know that the journey of 1,000 miles begins with a single step. What is equally important is understanding that the journey of 1,000 miles consists of THOUSANDS of single steps. Consistent action over time is how tiny plants grow through cracks in the concrete. They are inspired by the sunshine!

But what is the most effective and most appropriate action? Once you know where you are going, the next critical action is to simply take the next small step.

Going really hard in a the wrong direction will only get you further from where you want to go, faster. Now that you have clearly defined what it is that you want, decide what the next small step would be and take it.

I've heard it said that the "comfort zone" is a deadly place, and that the only way to get your goal is to step outside the comfort zone. But how often does this lead to an addiction to activity that has little or nothing to do with getting a result? Did you ever feel like you were working your ass off all the time, constantly doing something and never really seeming to make any headway toward the goal?

There is an enormous difference between being busy and being productive. Busy leads to "doing". Productive leads to "done".

How "hard you try" doesn't determine the result. In fact it often has little to do with the result and in many cases is counterproductive.

No Pain No Gain

You may be thinking "But being successful has to be hard, *right*? What about 'No Pain No Gain'??"

That is what we are taught; that success is synonymous with suffering... you have to work very hard, for long hours, no sleep, no time for fun....that you must become a martyr for your cause in order to achieve success. Why are we taught that? I believe it is because it is very easy to confuse *sacrifice* with *suffering*.

Suffering is the state of undergoing pain, distress, or hardship. Injury. Loss of a loved one. A house and it's contents burns. These things cause suffering. Think of the people in third world countries without adequate food or even clean water. If suffering = success then wouldn't they be among the most successful people in history?

The truth is, this idea of "no pain, no gain" is a limiting belief. It's a belief which will actually hold you back and prevent you from reaching your true potential. It is a self-imposed obstacle that creates problems where none actually exist.

But what about sacrifice?

Sacrifice the surrender or destruction of something prized or desirable for the sake of something considered as having a higher or more pressing claim. Or in other words, is giving up something of value for something of a higher value.

I love me some Star Wars. I have a cat named Skywalker. I went with a friend to see The Force Awakens the week it opened. I paid the extra cash to see it in IMAX 3-D. I sacrificed twenty something dollars (not including the cost of popcorn) in order to have a certain experience.

A few days later I saw it again with my wife Mandy and our niece and nephew. This time we saw it on a regular screen, no 3-D, for $7.50 each. For Mandy (who is not as much of a Star Wars fan as I am) it was not worth the extra cost to see it in IMAX 3-D. The difference in cost wasn't something she was willing to part with to have the experience. It wasn't worth the sacrifice to her.

Everything is subject to the universal law of cause and effect. Everything comes at a cost. Sacrifice is absolutely necessary for success, but that doesn't mean that it has to include needless pain and suffering. Once I understood that I not only didn't have to suffer for success, but that suffering is actually counter productive, it was incredibly liberating.

Suffering for your success is enduring something you don't want and isn't necessary. Sacrifice is willingly trading for an increase in value. What are you willing to give in exchange for what you want?

If you have the goal to get leaner, then the sacrifice will come in the form of trading junk food and inactivity for nutritious food and movement. You may have to sacrifice late nights watching TV in order to get up early and go to the gym.

If you have the goal of building a business, you may have to sacrifice money for education. Sacrifice is necessary. Suffering is optional.

Dissolve obstacles rather than break through them. This is the difference between focusing on the problem and focusing on the solution. How you get past the obstacle is not the important thing. Getting past it is. Sometimes it may not be so clear. That is when you ask the question:

Am I creating the results that I want?

So if how hard you try or the amount of effort isn't the key, then what is? The quality of your actions.

It doesn't matter how fast you drive if you are going the wrong way. Even if you are on the right road, it makes a lot of sense to release the parking break before you stomp on the gas pedal.

Stop focusing on how much effort you put into something and instead focus on the quality of the action. Dissolve the obstacles.

In all your actions strive for the highest possible quality. In doing this you ensure that every action that you take toward a given objective is the most effective, most efficient and most productive thing that you can do at that time to move you toward your goal.

Stop trying.

We are taught from a very early age that it is important to try. We are taught that the most important thing is not winning or losing, passing or failing, doing well or doing poorly. What matters is that we tried our hardest. What does this mean?

I checked the word "try" the dictionary and found three primary definitions-
  • to make an effort to do something; to attempt to accomplish or complete something
  • to do or use (something) in order to see if it works or will be successful
  • to do or use (something) in order to find out if you like it

If we look at these definitions we can see that they all have some sort of trial or test built in, and the distinct possibility of NOT having a favorable response.

In some cases trying may be the most important thing. For example, you have a beer that you love. I have never tasted it. I will try it. This is important work.

However, given the context it is commonly used in, more often than not, "trying harder" is not the answer. In fact, it is usually counterproductive. How can this be so? Everybody knows that the one who tries the hardest wins, right?

Let's put it to the test. I want you to do something for me, right now. Ready? Good.

Here we go: I want you to try to make your hair grow longer. Really try hard. Try as hard as you can. Go ahead, put as much effort into it as you possibly can...

Now, you can do that all day, every day and your hair will grow. Does that mean it worked? Clearly it did. You tried really really really hard and you were rewarded with longer hair.

But you see, your hair will also grow longer if you put ZERO effort into it.....as long as you don't cut it. It is not a matter of effort or trying. It is actually a matter of avoiding what is counter productive to your goal, of NOT doing the thing that will prevent you from achieving it.

These counter-productive activities can sometimes be the only thing that stand in the way of massive success. By doing these things, you are actually doing the OPPOSITE of your stated goal.

If at first you don't succeed....

Without having to ask you to do so, you almost certainly finished that sentence, didn't you? When we are kids we are taught this phrase. But is "try, try again" really the right answer? Maybe. Maybe not.

Are you smarter than a fly?

Did you ever see a fly that keeps slamming his little fly face against a window with all of his little fly might, trying over and over to get outside with all of the effort he can muster with his little fly wings? What if he flew a few feet over and out the window next to it, which is wide open? Freedom.

But instead he continues pounding against the same window, suffering, until his little fly body collapse and dies. He dies not from lack of effort, but from lack of awareness. He is 100% fully committed to his current plan. So much so, that he is not aware that there is another way. A way that ensures the success and freedom he seeks.

I prefer to live by "If at first you don't succeed, come up with a better plan!"

Suppose I hand you a metal spike and ask you to bend it, without using any tools, machines or equipment like a vise, could you do it? For most people the answer is "NO".

What if I showed you how to wrap it in leather to protect your skin from being punctured, how to hold it in your hands to get the best possible grip on it, how to position your body in order to maximize your leverage?

What if I demonstrate all of this by bending a spike for you, so that you can see it in action and know that it is possible for a another person to perform this feat? Could you do it then?

In my experience, for most people it is still a big fat "NO".

I have told you exactly what to do. I have shown you how to do it and demonstrated how it is done. Yet, you are still unable to do it. What if you just try harder? What if I tell you to visualize it with more detail?

This is exactly the problem that I have seen with most self-help programs. They are missing the steps between where you are now and where you want to be.

But what if I give you a plan, a way to practice and condition your body and get stronger over time? Do you think that following the plan over time, taking the many small steps, will eventually get you there? With habitual practice, effective action and very little trying, you will get there. I've coached many people to be able to this very thing, including my friend Joe Vitale.

Steel Fears Joe

10
DEVELOPING YOUR SUPER POWER

We all have busy lives. In order to change our results, we have to change our activities.

How can you structure your activities so that you are aligned with your worthy ideal? There are three important elements. Doing any one of these activities each day will help you move toward your worthy ideal. Doing two or all three of them carries even more power. Repetition is the mother of mastery.

Commit to doing these activities daily and you will be amazed. It will require discipline and commitment. You will have to plan things differently than you have done in the past. You will begin re-programming your subconscious mind with a purposeful image of your superhuman self. Remember, the subconscious doesn't make a distinction between the imagined and what exists in the physical world.

As the Mighty Atom said: *"Think that you are strong, and you are"*. But you can substitute any other ideal for the word "strong".

ACTION STEP ONE: STUDY
The verb study means "to apply oneself to the acquisition of knowledge, as by reading, investigation, or practice." Reading something once and then moving on is not study. We must

absorb the information, digest it and allow it to become a part of us. How do we do that?

The Super Power Hour.
Set aside one hour each day and use it to develop your super power.

One hour spent focused on your goal, five days per week is 260 hours in a year (if you take weekends off). That is the equivalent of six and a half 40 hour weeks in a year.

Schedule it to be around the same time each day. I have found that most people get the best results when it is the first thing they do in the morning. Wake up early and spend the first hour getting your mind going with all the wondrous possibilities of your worthy ideal. By doing this you are impressing it and your new super human self image onto your subconscious mind and setting the tone of success for the rest of the day.

Super power tasks:

Write it out
Daily rewriting of your vision statement. As we saw in the previous exercise, this is a very powerful way to impress your new conditioning on your subconscious mind. Writing causes thinking and the physical action of writing registers in your mind as action taken toward the goal.

Gratitude
Gratitude keeps you connected to the source of infinite supply. After you have written your primary goal or worthy ideal on at the top of the page, think of at least five things in

your life that make you feel grateful. What these things are doesn't matter as much as the emotion of gratitude they invoke.

Ideas

Go through as many ideas as you can that will move you toward your objective. Think of ideas that will help you to become, do, or have what you have set your mind upon. Relax and let the ideas flow through your mind and onto the page. At first this may seem strange or difficult. You will also notice that many of your ideas are no good. Like any new skill, it will require repetition to become competent.

As the ideas come to you, don't edit or censor. Let them come, even if they seem silly, far fetched, dumb or downright impossible. Let them flow, without interruption. Just put the ideas in writing. Later you can go through them to decide which ones are best.

Shoot for 10 ideas. If you get more that is great. If you don't, then that's fine too. Some of your ideas will be better than others and one really good idea is all you need to change your entire existence.

Some thoughts to spur your creative idea flow:
What can I do to move closer to the goal?
What is the next small step I can take today?
What can I eliminate that is hindering me?
What will I be like when I have achieved the goal?
Think as if you are already that person.
How does that person act?
How do they talk?
What do they do?

Who do they associate with?

What changes do you need to make to become that person? As you do this, you will incrementally begin living out the visualization until you have become the person you want to be.

Affirmation

Reading and re-reading your worthy ideal many times throughout the day will keep your mind focused on it. You will find that ideas continue to come to you or you will think of better ways to execute previous ideas that you have had. Affirmation acts like a GPS for you worthy ideal. It guides you in the direction of the goal.

Other activities

Daily reading, listening to audio or watching video of material that relates to your worthy ideal is a huge advantage we have in the information age. Read books and articles, listen to interviews with experts or mentors. Watch videos and listen to podcasts. Just be certain that all of this is supporting your quest, not distracting you from it.

ACTION STEP TWO: PRACTICE

There is a really old joke about a violinist who arrived in New York City for a concert performance at the legendary venue, Carnegie Hall.

The musician, carrying his violin in it's case, asks another guy walking down the street:

"How do you get to Carnegie Hall?"

The other guy replies "PRACTICE!!"

The verb practice means "to exercise oneself by repeated performance in order to acquire skill".

There is a popular saying that I am certain that you have heard. Fill in the bank if you know the answer:

Practice makes _____.

If you are like most people, you said "perfect". And you are wrong. Or at least not as accurate as you could be. The very clever person will read this and agree, then follow up with "*PERFECT* practice makes perfect." That's closer, but I still think it can be better.

There are two problems with this statement.

First, it implies that you already know how to do it perfectly.

Second, it implies that all you have to do is repeat it the same way to improve, which is another way to say "more is better".

Paraphrasing my friend Adam Glass: More is NOT better. Better is better. Then Better becomes More.

I believe that the most accurate way to say it is: Practice makes PERMANENT.

If you understand that practice is done with the intent of improving skill, then you will always get better. If you practice poorly, you become more effective and efficient at doing it poorly.

Repetition is the mother of mastery. Daily practice yields results. The amount of repetition and the sheer effort doesn't determine the result, it is the quality of the effort that matters.

The better the quality of the action, the more efficient it is. Get more done with less. In all actions, strive for the highest possible quality of action, knowing that the more efficient you are the more effective you are.

Seek not to put as much effort into your action (trying) but rather to put as much quality into your actions. In doing this, you ensure that every action you take is the most effective, most efficient and most productive thing that you can do at that time to move you toward your goal.

The daily practice of the activities and skills on the following pages will propel you in the direction of your goal.

VISUALIZATION
This is a bit of a misnomer, because when done to maximum effect ALL of your senses are involved, not just vision. I sometimes call it "imagining" or simply "imaging". Napoleon

Hill referred to it as autosuggestion and Joe Vitale calls is "Nevillizing". This comes from Neville Goddard, who said:

"If there is something tonight that you really want in this world, then experience in imagination what you would experience in the flesh were you to realize your goal, and then deafen your ears, and blind your eyes to all that denies the reality of your assumption." – Neville Goddard, 1948

What you call it is not that important. The important thing is to know that by engaging as many of your senses as possible and making it as real in your mind as you can, the subconscious believes that the visualization, the fantasy, is how things are in reality. This will begin to shift you into living as if it has already happened. As you become more practiced, you will make some changes to personalize it, but the general principles will always apply.

Repetition is the mother of mastery. I know I wrote that already. See how it works? Set aside 20-30 minutes 2-3 times per day to relax and visualize. Immediately before going to bed at night and when you wake up in the morning for your Super Power Hour are fantastic times.

In the study section we talked about a daily rewrite and multiple readings of your goal statement or worthy ideal. You cannot overdo this. The same thing applies to visualization. At a minimum, you will read your statement and visualize in the morning and at night before going to sleep. If you can fit it in during your day at other times, that is even better. Utilize the power of your imagination to create an experience in your mind.

RELAX: MEDITATION 101

Mediation means different things to different people. My training has roots in martial art and yoga. I know some people who have had fantastic results with various smart phone apps, which is completely foreign to me. You don't have to hole up in a cave, chant or use an app. For our purposes here, meditation is simply entering into a relaxed state, on purpose.

In order for the imagination to work at maximum effectiveness, you must become as relaxed as possible. Creative energy flows better through a relaxed medium. I have a near-daily meditation practice and almost all the truly successful people I know do as well, even if they don't call it that. Successful people know how to be relaxed.

The two primary ingredients of all useful meditation practices are deep breathing and a calm mind. Here is an entry-level process to get you started:

Choose a place where you will not be distracted. Find a comfortable position either sitting or lying down. Relax.

Remember how we said "trying" doesn't work? This is a fantastic example of that. Do not "try" to relax. Trying = effort. Relaxing = lack of tension and effort. You cannot put effort into being effortless.

Once you are in the meditative position that you like the most, close your eyes and slow your breathing. Put your tongue against the roof of your mouth, right behind the front teeth. This ancient chi kung (qigong) practice will help you to keep your face and jaw relaxed.

Focus on your breath. Make it deep, seamless and smooth. Think of directing your breath all the way down to your feet and filling your body as if it were an empty vessel. You may find it useful to count, for example inhale for a count of 6 and exhale for a count of 6. You could use 4 or 5 or 10.....the focus on the breath is what matters, not the numbers.

Deliberately put a smile on your face. Tighten up your toes for several seconds and then release them. Repeat this three times. As you feel the tension leaving your toes, notice the relaxed feeling that occurs. Bring the relaxed feeling into your ankles and calves by tensing and relaxing them the same way. Continue up to your knees and thighs, allowing yourself to soften and relax. With each exhale, let go of a little more tension. See the tension leaving your body with each breath. You will probably feel yourself sinking deeper into your position as you allow the the tension to leave.

See yourself as a hollow vessel, like a cup or vase. Picture your torso filling up with relaxation. Let your belly and lower back fill up. Allow the relaxation to flow up into your chest, upper back, and shoulders. Let it overflow into your arms and down to your finger tips, filling your arms.

Let the relaxed feeling move up the back of your head and around your neck, up over your ears and the top of your head to rest behind your eyes. "Catch" the feeling with your relaxed tongue, mix it with your saliva, and swallow it down to the bottom of your belly. Feel your entire body in this deeply relaxed state. Repeat this whole filling up process three or more times.

Revel in the relaxed feeling. This is the foundational exercise for meditation. You can do it as a standalone exercise to practice getting and staying relaxed.

This is also the first section of the next exercise on visualization. Move straight into the next exercise or you can finish up here.

To finish, simply bring your awareness back to your surroundings, becoming more and more energized with each breath. When you are ready, open your eyes and go on about your day.

VISUALIZATION EXERCISE

When you are fully relaxed, see yourself standing at the top of a staircase with 10 stairs. Slowly begin to walk down the stairs, becoming more relaxed with each successive step. Once you are at the bottom you will be completely relaxed.

See yourself standing in front of a door. Open the door and enter the room. You are now inside your own private movie theater, with a giant screen.

Take your seat and see the image of your superhuman self projected onto the screen in your mind. Make it as real an experience as you possibly can. Become emotionally involved. Hear the sounds. Now project yourself from your seat *into the movie,* imagining yourself doing and acting like the person you will become, with all the senses. See and feel yourself making the actual physical and mechanical execution of the steps involved, just as I described in my Red Nail visualization.

When you are ready, return to the doorway and come back up the stairs. With each step, you become more and more aware of your surroundings. Once you reach the top of the stairs, open your eyes and be fully present in your body.

There are countless stories of top-level athletes who practice visualizing themselves smoothly and easily playing their game. They see themselves on the podium, holding their trophy or medal. Remember, the subconscious mind makes no distinction between real and imagined. As you practice relaxed visualization, you are programming the subconscious with a new pattern of conditioning. The subconscious will direct your behavior in a way that matches this new conditioning and your super power will develop.

ACTION STEP THREE: SHARE

Share means "to allow someone to use or enjoy something that one possesses".

This is exactly what it sounds like. I am of the opinion that in order to truly master something you must be able to communicate it to others. Besides that, your super power, your worthy ideal most certainly contains some element that will help other people live fuller, happier lives.

"You are a creative center, from which increase is given off to all.

Be sure of this, and convey assurance of the fact to every man, woman, and child with whom you come in contact. No matter how small the transaction, even if it be only the selling of a stick of candy to a little child, put into it the thought of increase, and make sure that the customer is impressed with the thought.

Convey the impression of advancement with everything you do, so that all people shall receive the impression that you are an Advancing Man, and that you advance all who deal with you."- Wallace Wattles, The Science of Getting Rich

In everything you do, do it with the intent of leaving others with the "impression of increase". Make it so that all the interactions that people have with you leave them affected in some way that improves the quality of their life. This is the fundamental idea behind it being better to give than to receive, because it is through giving that we open up the channels of circulation. Through these channels good intention creates an upward spiral of success for everyone.

With the technology of today, the world is a small place and you have the ability to reach millions of people from your keyboard. Here are a few ways that you can share and circulate your worthy ideal:

Write

Start a blog. It is incredibly easy to set up a blog. You can do it for little or no cost with a simple wordpress site and have a platform to spread your message. You can even use affiliate programs to sell products and earn money. I am not an expert on this, but I know that there are many programs out there that can teach you all you need to know.

Social media

We live in an age where almost everyone uses Facebook, twitter, instagram and many other platforms to connect with people around the world. Much of what makes it onto social media does little or nothing to leave the impression of increase. You can change that for the people on your friends list. By the way, if you want to follow me, I am @irontamer on twitter and instagram (or simply, the 'gram, as my wife calls it.) My Facebook professional page is Iron Tamer Dave Whitley and my youtube channel is Iron Tamer.

Video, audio, etc

Speaking of YouTube, you can set one up for yourself, if you don't enjoy writing. You could also start a podcast. Put your message out there for the world to absorb.

Communicate your message to others in personal interaction.

You don't have to limit yourself to online communication, of course. In any conversation you have, you can find a way to inject your super power into it. You might wind up leading a class of some sort. It all depends on your dream.

List other ideas that you have for sharing your message:

_____

_____

_____

_____

_____

_____

_____

_____

_____

_____

_____

_____

_____

_____

_____

_____

_____

_____

_____

_____

_____

_____

_____

_____

NAPOLEON HILL'S FORMULA FOR SUCCESS

The final exercise I am sharing with you is directly adapted from Napoleon Hill's *Think and Grow Rich*. It will teach you to keep your desired goal a priority in your life.

You must dedicate yourself not only to a plan, but to HABITS.

1.   Fix in your mind the exact qualities that you want to improve.   Be definite in your mind.   Create vivid mental pictures of your goal. You did this in the previous exercise. If it is increased income, for example, decide on the exact amount you want to earn. If it is weight loss, or weight lifted, decide on the exact amount. This goal is YOUR goal. I encourage you to go big with it. Bigger than what seems possible. You don't need to know how you are going to do it. You only need to DECIDE that you WILL.

2.   Determine exactly what you intend to GIVE in return for what you desire.   There is no such thing as something for nothing. Isaac Newton's 3rd law- for every action there is an equal and opposite reaction- applies to this situation.

Another way to think of this is that there is no such thing as something for nothing.   There is a universal Law of Sowing and Reaping. In order to have, do or become the thing you want, you must be willing to do the things that go along with having, doing and becoming that thing. This is where the sacrifice comes in. We must be willing to pay the price.

What is that price? The specifics depend on the goal you have chosen, but the common factor is that you will have to get into the habit of focusing your intention on what you want, instead of what you do not want. Whenever thoughts of fear or doubt creep into your mind, be ready to replace them with thoughts of your completed goal. Sacrifice means giving up something of a lesser value for something of a greater value. Develop the habit of giving or doing more than is expected.

3. Establish a definite date for when you plan to possess the desired objective, keeping in mind that "Nature, to be commanded, must first be obeyed.", as Sir Francis Bacon said.

4. Create a definite plan for carrying out your desire and begin at once. Whether or not you are ready really doesn't matter. Your plan will evolve as you do.

5. Together with your clear, concise statement of the qualities you want to acquire, name a time limit, state what you intend to give to reach your goals, and describe clearly the plan for which you intend to accumulate it.

6. As you read your written statement aloud each morning, see, feel and believe yourself already in possession of these qualities.

It is vitally important to follow these instructions to the letter. When you do, you are programing your subconscious mind to focus on the destination and by repeating it daily, you are constantly reminding yourself to stay on track.

When you drive, you are constantly making small adjustments of the steering wheel to stay on the road or to navigate traffic. If you keep you hand on the wheel, it is easy to stay on course. If you let go of the wheel, though, you will quickly start to head in a direction you didn't plan to go. Keep your hands off the wheel too long and you wind up in the ditch, or worse. Daily reading of your desire acts exactly the same way. It keeps you on course with minor adjustments.

Here is the example of the process that Hill detailed in Think and Grow Rich.

"First- Go into some quiet spot (preferably in bed at night) where you will not be disturbed or interrupted, close your eyes, and repeat aloud, (so you may hear your own words) the written statement of the amount of money you intend to accumulate, the time limit for its accumulation, and a description of the service or merchandise you intend to give in return for the money. As you carry out these instructions, SEE YOURSELF ALREADY IN POSSESSION OF THE MONEY.

For example:--Suppose that you intend to accumulate $50,000 by the first of January, five years hence, that you intend to give personal services in return for the money, in the capacity of a salesman. Your written statement of your purpose should be similar to the following:

"By the first day of January, (of whatever year you have chosen), I will have in my possession $50,000, which will come to me in various amounts from time to time during the interim. In return for this money I will give the most efficient service of which I am capable, rendering the fullest possible quantity, and the best possible quality of service in the capacity of salesman of . . . . (describe the service or merchandise you intend to sell).

"I believe that I will have this money in my possession. My faith is so strong that I can now see this money before my eyes. I can touch it with my hands. It is now awaiting transfer to me at the time, and in the proportion that I deliver the service I intend to render in return for it. I am awaiting a plan by which to accumulate this money, and I will follow that plan, when it is received."

Second- Repeat this program night and morning until you can see, (in your imagination) the money you intend to accumulate.

Third- Place a written copy of your statement where you can see it night and morning, and read it just before retiring, and upon arising until it has been memorized.

Remember, as you carry out these instructions, that you are applying the principle of auto-suggestion, for the purpose of giving orders to your subconscious mind. Remember, also, that your subconscious mind will act ONLY upon instructions which are emotionalized, and handed over to it with "feeling."

FAITH is the strongest, and most productive of the emotions. Follow the instructions given in the chapter on FAITH.

These instructions may, at first, seem abstract. Do not let this disturb you. Follow the instructions, no matter how abstract or impractical they may, at first, appear to be. The time will soon come, if you do as you have been instructed, in spirit as well as in act, when a whole new universe of power will unfold to you."

Of course, this process works for any goal you may have and is not limited to financial gain. It is up to you choose something worthy of you. Something superhuman.

COMMITMENT

"Every one of us is the sum total of our own thoughts. He is where he is because that's exactly where we really want or feel we deserve to be, whether we'll admit that or not.

Each of us must live off the fruit of his thoughts in the future, because what you think today and tomorrow, next month and next year, will mold your life and determine your future. You're guided by your mind." -Earl Nightingale

The exercises in this book will keep your objective ever-present in your conscious mind, which will in time re-program your subconscious conditioning and make the accomplishment of your goal and your super human development a mathematical certainty. It is vital that you make a binding commitment with yourself to see it through. When you sign your name below, do it with the same seriousness as you would if you were entering into any legal agreement. Your word is your bond.

I commit to carry out the exercises in this book every day for 90 days. I commit to allocate a special time each day and will train myself to use that time for daily action steps toward the development of my super human self.

_____

Name

_____

Date

CONCLUSION

I encourage you to apply this formula to whatever goal you have in your marvelous mind. What can you expect?

Do it for 90 days and you'll be astounded by the progress you make. Do it every day for a year and you will most certainly change your life for the better in practically every area.

The time is going to pass anyway. You are going to be doing something anyway.

Everything you see around you….buildings, cars, computers, smart phones, the internet, the lightbulb…..originated as a thought. Someone imagined it. Someone developed a plan and carried it out to completion.

The twisted horse shoes and bent steel that are left over at the end of my strongman shows are testament to it in my own life.

They began as a thought, a goal, a worthy ideal. So are the words you are reading now.

What can you do if you decide to purposefully take control of your own thoughts?

What can you accomplish if you act in harmony with the definite purpose, that burning desire?

Anything and everything you want, that's what.

Now go forth, and kick much ass.......

ABOUT THE AUTHOR

Iron Tamer Dave Whitley is a motivational speaker and strongman based in Nashville, TN. He first became interested in strength as a kid, reading comic books and dreaming of becoming superhuman. Dave has performed all over the US and internationally. He was featured in the German documentary Kraftakt, a film about strength.

He performs astounding feats of strength such as:
• bending steel bars, spikes and wrenches
• tearing decks of cards
• twisting horse shoes
• driving a nail through a board with his hand
• breaking chains
• leveraging sledghammers

The feats he performs are used as an illustration of the mindset needed to accomplish the impossible. His purpose is to inspire the audience to leave their limitations behind and become the greatest possible version of themselves.

Visit his website www.irontamer.com
Follow him on social media:
@irontamer on twitter
@irontamer on instagram
Iron Tamer Dave Whitley on Facebook.
Iron Tamer on YouTube

NOTES

NOTES

NOTES

Made in the USA
Lexington, KY
01 September 2017